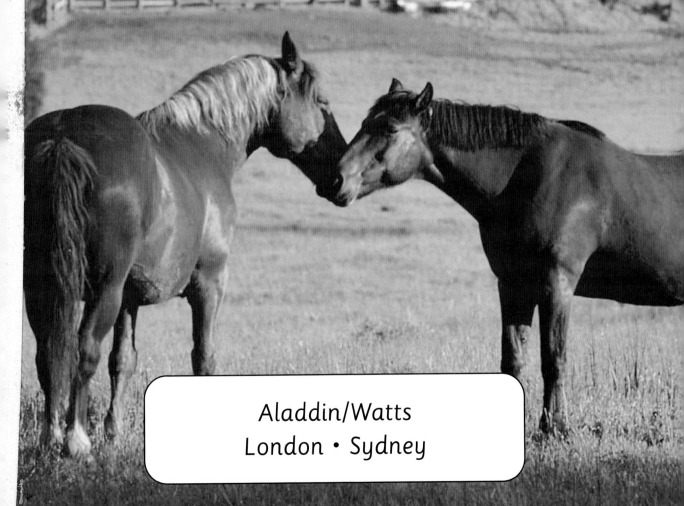

Read and Play
Horses

by Jim Pipe

Aladdin/Watts
London • Sydney

horse

2

These are **horses**.

Horses run fast.

3

body

4

A horse has a big **body**.

It likes to roll over.

5

legs

A horse has four **legs**.

6

hoof

A horse's feet are **hooves**.

7

head

A horse has a big **head**.

8

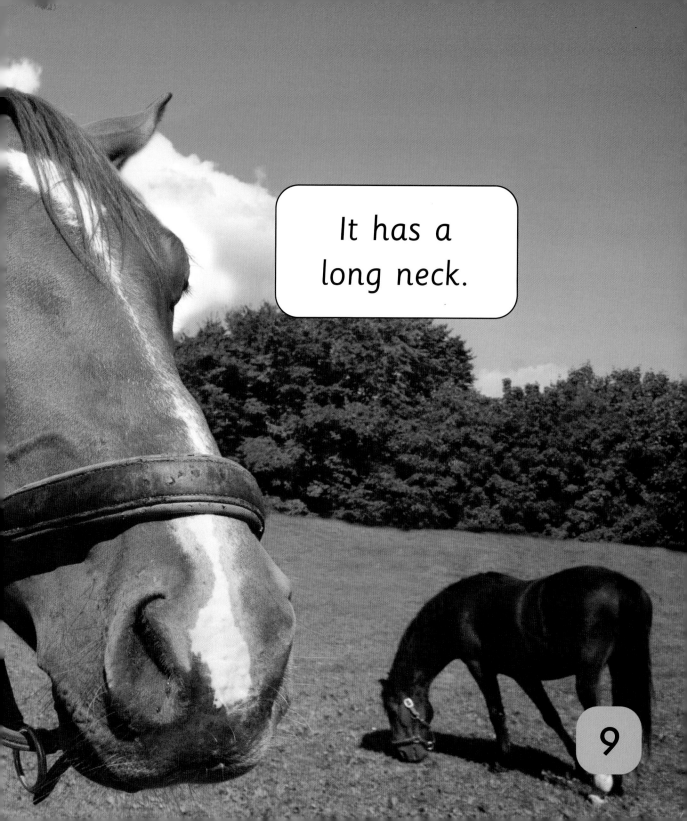

mane

A horse has a **mane**.

10

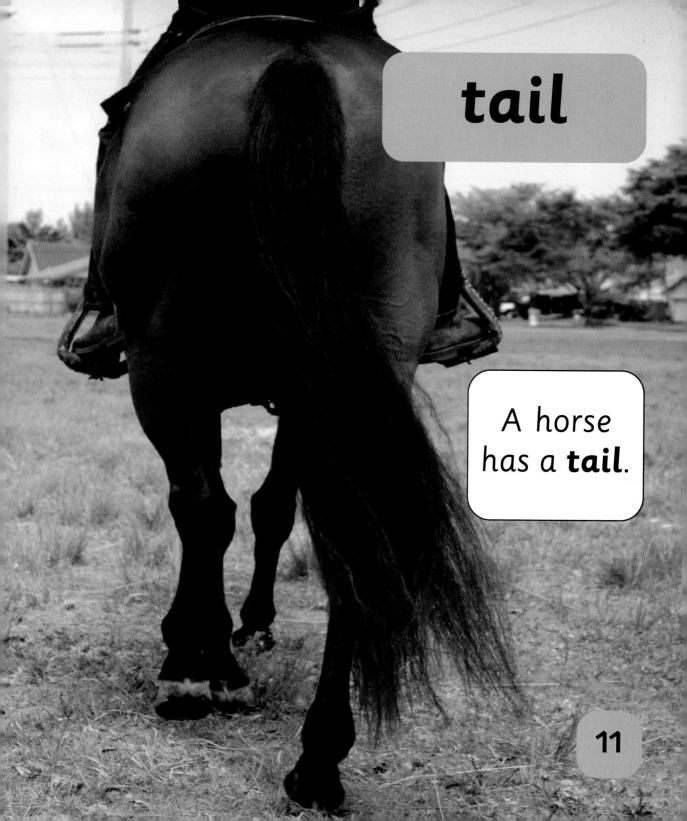

tail

A horse
has a **tail**.

11

grass

12

A horse eats **grass**.

A horse drinks water.

13

foal

14

A baby horse is a **foal**.

A **foal** has long legs.

15

pony

A **pony** is a small horse.

16

Cart horses are big!

17

ride

18 A cowboy **rides** a horse.

jump

A horse can **jump**.

19

What is it?

foal

tail

hoof

mane

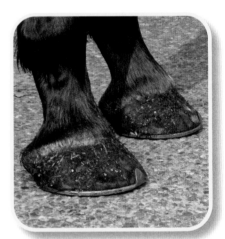

20 Match the words and pictures.

How many?

Can you count the horses?

21

What colour?

black

white

spots

brown

22 Match the colour to the horse.

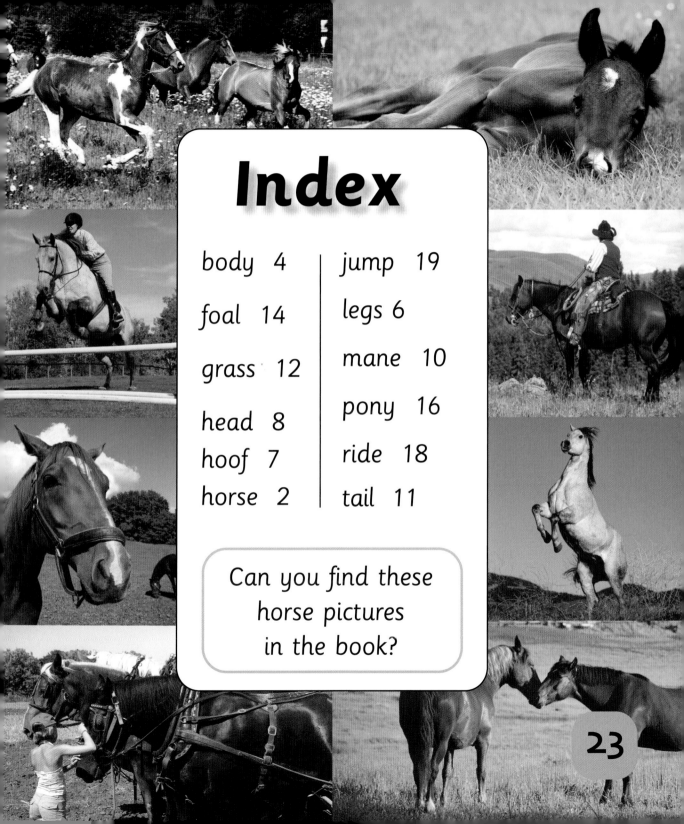

Index

body 4

foal 14

grass 12

head 8

hoof 7

horse 2

jump 19

legs 6

mane 10

pony 16

ride 18

tail 11

Can you find these
horse pictures
in the book?

For Parents and Teachers

Questions you could ask:

p. 2 How many horses can you see? Six.
When horses run fast we say they gallop.
p. 4 What is this horse doing? Rolling on its back,
to scratch an itch or keep its coat clean.
p. 7 What sound do hooves make? "Clip-clop".
Hooves are protected by metal shoes – you can see
the horseshoes clearly on pages 4-5.
p. 9 What does a horse have on its head?
Eyes, ears, nostrils, mouth. Unlike humans,
horses have their eyes on the side of their head.
p. 11 What other animals have a tail? Squirrel, dog,
cat etc. Horses use their tail to swat away flies.
p. 12 Where does a horse live? These horses are
out in the fields. A stable is a home for horses at
night and during the winter (see picture on page 21).
p. 14 What is this foal doing?
Resting. Baby animals need lots of rest.
p. 17 What does a horse's coat feel like? Soft/smooth.
Compare with other animals, e.g. fur, scales, feathers.

p. 18 What is the cowboy sitting on? A saddle.
A saddle helps riders to stay on a horse. Riders pull
on the reins to make a horse turn left or right.

Activities you could do:

• Make lucky horseshoes – cut them from card
then wrap them in aluminium foil. They can also
be used to play horseshoes (pitched at a stick).
• Play a game of "pin the tail on the donkey/horse "
using a blindfold and a picture of a horse.
• Help the reader to build a stable for horses from
a cardboard box, e.g. with a stable door.
• Encourage the reader to act out riding a horse
(sitting back to front in chair), pretending to hold reins
and using commands such as "whoa" and "gee up".
• Ask the reader to colour in outline of a horse,
copying horses from this book, e.g. skewbald on
pages 2-3, chestnut on page 9, or perhaps zebra stripes.
• Read aloud a horse story, such as Black Beauty,
Pegasus the winged horse or the Trojan Horse.

© Aladdin Books Ltd 2006

Designed and produced by
Aladdin Books Ltd
2/3 Fitzroy Mews
London W1T 6DF

First published in 2006
by Franklin Watts
338 Euston Road
London NW1 3BH

Franklin Watts Australia
Hachette Children's Books
Level 17/207 Kent Street
Sydney NSW 2000

ISBN 0 7496 6866 0

A catalogue record for
this book is available
from the British Library.

Dewey Classification:
636.1

Printed in Malaysia

All rights reserved

Series consultant
Zoe Stillwell is an experienced
Early Years teacher currently
teaching at Pewley Down Infant
School, Guildford.

Photocredits:
l-left, r-right, b-bottom, t-top,
c-centre, m-middle
All photos from istockphoto.com
except: 1, 18, 23 mtl & bl — Corel.
6, 23mbl — Corbis. 16, 22bl –
Select Pictures.